Teaching Is...

Moments that Inspire and Motivate
Teachers to Make a Difference

Written by
MARJAN GLAVAC

Teaching Is...
Moments that Inspire and Motivate
Teachers to Make A Difference

Marjan Glavac

Published by Marjan Glavac
wwwTheBusyEducator.com

Title: *Teaching Is: Moments that Inspire and Motivate Teachers to Make a Difference*
Format: Paperback
This publication has been assigned: 978-0-9683310-1-9

Title: *Teaching Is: Moments that Inspire and Motivate Teachers to Make a Difference*
Format: Hardcover book
This publication has been assigned: 978-0-9683310-0-2

Cover Design: Dianna Little
Cover and Interior Images: © Photodisc
Interior Design and Formatting: Dianna Little / Ryan Ashcroft

To Mr. John Ramsay
Teacher, Neighbor, Mentor

Veteran educator Marjan Glavac's latest book gives new meaning to the concept of the teachable moment. His collection of personal and inspirational affirmations are guaranteed to connect with anyone who has dedicated their lives to students in a classroom. For every educator who has felt frustrated, unappreciated, and overwhelmed, Teaching Is... reinforces the power of teachers to inspire, motivate, and make a difference.

This small book with a big message gotes beyond the curriculum, celebrating what true education is all about. New teachers will be reassured by the personal wisdom of an experienced educator who has walked the path before them; veteran teachers will feel refreshed and invigorated by the unbounded optimism and truthful insight.

This book is for every educator at any stage of their career. For parents and students who wish to acknowledge and thank the dedicated teachers who have made an impact with their caring guidance, Teaching Is... is the perfect and lasting gift.

Read. Enjoy. And share it with those who have made a difference in your life.

For free resources for getting a teaching job, becoming an effective teacher and making teaching fun, visit:

www.TheBusyEducator.com

Teaching Is...

Having students test you...

every day of the school year.

Teaching Is...

You immediately understand why a student behaves a certain way after meeting his or her parents.

Teaching Is...

At the end of a long week, leaving an empty classroom, walking down an empty hallway and leaving an empty school for a lonely car in the parking lot...yours.

Teaching Is...

After telling the class that you grew up without a microwave, a student asks "How did you reheat your food?" (You're tempted to say "Over the fire!")

Teaching Is...

Attending a high school awards ceremony and seeing your former elementary students receive top honors and awards for their accomplishments ...when a parent taps you on the shoulder and says, "You had a hand in this."

Teaching Is...

That incredible, indescribable feeling of relief when the last report card is written.

Teaching Is...

Getting a hug from the toughest student in your class on the last day of school...when no one else is looking.

Teaching Is...

During the last hours of a Friday afternoon while all of the students are working enthusiastically on an art project, and you're conferencing with a student, when out of the corner of your eye you notice your principal quietly standing in the doorway watching your class and smiling.

Teaching Is...

Having a student come up with a better way to solve a math problem, even though you've taught the same lesson for 5 years.

Teaching Is...

In the middle of a wonderful fantastic and well prepared lesson...fire drills, tornado drills, and lockdowns.

Teaching Is...

That one student, that thorn in your side, that constant pain, who doesn't come to class for one day...two days...three days...and secretly embarrassed that you're very happy.

Teaching Is...

Convinced that you have the worst class of your career, you come to class one day and find all your students have dressed up with a tie just like you.

Teaching Is...

Going to the fair and seeing students pet a farm animal for the very first time.

Teaching Is...

Trying to teach on Wacky Hair Day, Hawaiian Day, Backwards Day, Beach Day, Twin Day...

Teaching Is...

When your car stalls in the middle of a busy street and a former student you barely recognize but still remember as being selfish and uncaring, stops and magically starts your car and leaves as quietly and unassuming as he came.

Teaching Is...

Being told years and years later by students that you're still their favorite teacher.

Teaching Is...

During a class meeting to discuss bullying, when out of the blue, one student apologizes to another student for bullying her a year ago, then another student apologizes, then another and the tears of gratitude from the victim start pouring out like water from a broken dam...and from you as well.

Teaching Is...

Having a parent drop by who reinforces everything you just told the class about the importance of setting goals, doing your best in school and the importance of a good education.

Teaching Is...

A voice over the Public Address system asking YOU to come see the principal in her office...and the whole class shouts out "ooooooooooooooo".

Teaching Is...

Students who remind you that it's their birthday...

weeks in advance.

Teaching Is...

Always thinking about your curriculum, your students, your classroom...even when you're on holidays.

Teaching Is...

Frantically looking for that essential handout, that parent permission form, that test you wanted to give during the last period on a Friday that you spent hours making...and finding it weeks later under a pile of papers on your desk.

Teaching Is...

Being remembered and thanked at the end of the year...with a handwritten note on a scrap piece of wrinkled paper.

Teaching Is...

Spilling three boxes of hundreds of tiny blocks and manipulatives and having your students pick them up... without you asking them.

Teaching Is...

Being surprised by screams of joy in the middle of your lesson and seeing students rush to the windows to see big fluffy flakes of winter's first snow.

Teaching Is...

Working very late in your portable classroom, when you hear a knock at the door: a parent has made supper for you.

Teaching Is...

Being visited by a former student who tells you you're the best teacher he's ever had because you didn't lose your temper when he became frustrated and threw a desk at you and you never yelled at him all year...all the while you're quietly thinking it was because you never wanted to get him angry.

Teaching Is...

Watching a stream of refugees on the news one summer day and teaching one of them who arrives in your class in September how to catch a football, throw a baseball and bounce a basketball for the very first time in her life.

Teaching Is...

Asking your principal to listen to a child assessed 3 years below grade level read to him in his office and showing him the text the student will be reading... and then naming the student and seeing the look of amazement onyour principal's face.

Teaching Is...

Prepping your students on the importance to study for their final exam every day for a week...and then forgetting to bring the exams from home.

Teaching Is...

Telling an elementary student that one day she will become an Olympic athlete...and she does as a member of 2 Olympic teams.

Teaching Is...

Learning NEVER to put your coffee cup near any important papers on your desk...especially when you teach a class of overactive children.

Teaching Is...

Having a healing circle for your disruptive, disrespectful, out of control class, and learning that they just want to be heard...and loved.

Teaching Is...

Soon after telling students the importance of reading carefully every word for an assignment, and finding out that you didn't read the math sheet instructions carefully before assigning it.

Teaching Is...

"Mr. Glavac...Mr. Glavac...Mr. Glavac..."

"Yes, Michael?"

"Guess what Mr. Glavac? Guess what Mr. Glavac?"

"What, Michael?"

..."I forget."

Teaching Is...

When checking student monthly goal assignments, you notice a student who wrote down "focus" as his monthly goal...but forgot to put his name on his paper.

Teaching Is...

You intervene on behalf of a female student in your class whose brother bullies her mercilessly only to find 5 years later that the brother is your teenage son's best friend and stands by him when he is bullied.

Teaching Is...

Seeing students leaning forward in their seats, listening to your every word, following your each and every instruction, staring at you intently, mouths and eyes wide open...the AHA moment...something every teacher strives for.

Teaching Is...

Timing your washroom visits to the recess bell ...and training your bladder to hold it in between bells.

Teaching Is...

Finding out what you know and don't know

...really fast.

Teaching Is...

Telling a single parent of a difficult, high-needs, and stress inducing student, that he's made so much progress you can truthfully and sincerely say "It's been a pleasure teaching your son."

Teaching Is...

While watching a movie that you've seen a dozen times before, a student looks your way and asks, "Mr. Glavac...Mr. Glavac, are you sleeping?"
You reply, "No, just resting my eyes!"

Teaching Is...

Carrying a student suffering from Multiple Sclerosis from a portable classroom to the main school knowing he is going to die soon...and there's nothing you can do to prevent it.

Teaching Is...

Anxiously waiting and silently praying that the bus shows up for your end-of-the-year field trip.

Teaching Is...

Receiving a "Pat on the Back" from an administrator you respect, admire, and love.

Teaching Is...

Fondly remembering the student who gave you your 1st Christmas decoration in your first year of teaching...over 29 years ago.

Teaching Is...

Reluctantly lending a student $1.29 in February, writing it off as a bad loan, then seeing a neatly piled stack of coins on your desk on the last day of school.

Teaching Is...

Coaching a student lacking skills and confidence and seeing her score the game winning point.

Teaching Is...

Instead of "an apple a day" your students give you moose, Vietnamese spring rolls, Lebanese falafels, Greek moussaka, and Indian samosas.

Teaching Is...

Having a 12 year old student learn about his adoption and announce it publicly for the very first time in an oral presentation to his classmates.

Teaching Is...

Spending hours handwriting student report cards, sending them home then realizing you forgot to make copies for your files.

Teaching Is...

Inspiring a student to travel the world...

after hearing your travel stories in class.

Teaching Is...

Having a student apologize to you, by e-mail...20 years after you taught her.

Teaching Is...

Winning the district chess tournament by a single point scored in the last game of the tournament by the student you wanted to kick off the team because of poor behavior.

Teaching Is...

A class that all day long has "ants in their pants" and then in the last hour of the day, they listen to you attentively for over 40 minutes.

Teaching Is...

Snow days.

Teaching Is...

Having two antagonistic students, one male, one female, one white, one black, constantly at each other's throats since September, continuously provoking, belittling each other and refusing to be in each other's group. One day the boy finds a lost iPod and then quietly gives it back to that girl.

Teaching Is...

During a power outage, students use their Nintendo DS lite video games to light up the black board for fellow students to see the assignments.

Teaching Is...

Tirelessly promoting the importance of reading over and over again to a 10 year old student who still refuses to read...then 5 years later your non reader walks into your class and shows you the trilogy of fantasy books that he's proudly reading and thanks you for turning him on to reading.

Teaching Is...

Coming back from March Break rested, rejuvenated and relaxed...unable to remember the names of your worst students.

Teaching Is...

A student in tears over losing her house key...
finding it in her shoe.

Teaching Is...

An excited student celebrating her first double digit birthday...while you're very quietly celebrating one of those special birthdays that end in a "0".

Teaching Is...

Overflowing lost and found boxes with orphaned clothing and belongings that students never seem to remember having lost.

Teaching Is...

Watching your older students teach their younger
Kindergarten "buddies" how to read, print, and do
addition.

Teaching Is...

Playing touch football and soccer with your students...in the snow.

Teaching Is...

Enjoying hot chocolate with your students after playing touch football and soccer in the snow.

Teaching Is...

Turning off all the classroom lights and asking students to close their eyes, close their mouths and put their hands over their ears and then telling them that this is how Helen Keller lived her entire life.

Teaching Is...

Coffee...lots and lots of coffee!

Teaching Is...

Seeing a student who struggled all year finally "getting it".

Teaching Is...

Angrily filling out an office referral form for a student who blew up, melted down and swore at you, only to realize...it was your fault. You rip up the referral form and repair the relationship with the student.

Teaching Is...

You're waiting in line for a movie, waiting to be served in a restaurant, walking through a store and you see curious stares from a number of people, and you hear the words "It's Mr. Glavac".

Teaching Is...

You can tell if it's a full moon or if a storm is coming without ever going outside.

Teaching Is...

Never, never, ever giving up on a student.

Teaching Is...

Stopping yourself and thinking twice before disciplining other parent's children in public.

Teaching Is...

Leaving school on a late Friday night exhausted, but knowing deep down that you made a difference.

Who is Marjan Glavac?

Marjan Glavac is a best selling author, speaker and elementary classroom teacher with over 29 years of teaching experience. He has taught inner city students, students with emotional/behavioral disorders, ESL, and IEP students. Marjan is a dynamic international speaker and workshop presenter having spoken to thousands of teachers. His customized keynotes have included the following topics: Chalk Board Lessons From The Digital Age; Going Beyond The Rainbow (Or How To Be A Great Teacher); Burn Bright or Burn Out - Motivating Teachers for Life and his newest keynote based on his book: Teaching Is...Moments That Inspire And Motivate Teachers To Make A Difference.

Marjan is the author of 4 books: The Busy Educator's Guide To The World Wide Web 1st and 2nd Editions, How To Make A Difference: Inspiring Students To Do Their Best, Teaching Is...Moments That Inspire And Motivate Teachers To Make A Difference and co-creator of How to Thrive and Survive in Your Classroom teleseminar.

Marjan is also the creator of one of the Internet's longest running free teacher monthly newsletters: The Busy Educator's Newsletter (1998). He is also the recipient of the following teacher awards:

- **The Prime Minister's Award for Excellence in Teaching**
- **Mathematics, Science and TechnologyThe Roberta Bondar (first Canadian female astronaut) Award for Science and Technology.**
- **The National Institute Award for Excellence in Teaching.**
- **The Roy C. Hill Award for Educational Innovation.**
- **A Certificate of Merit from TVO (Canadian equivalent to PBS)**

Throughout his career, Marjan has used humor, story-telling and unique teaching methods to motivate his students. He's tested egg drop projects by dropping them from the school rooftop, incorporated chess concepts to teach students about consequences, utilized shoes to teach accountability, integrated role play and cooking to make the curriculum come to life. He has also taught about globalization with dozens of telecommunications projects involving students from K-University on every continent of the world. His students have been involved in projects sponsored by Global SchoolNet Foundation, Kidlink, Academy One, CCCnet, AT&T Japan, Lycos and in the creation of the NewsOntario online newspaper project. His K-8 students have also participated in e-mail, travel buddy, research projects and polishing mirrors for the NASA Starshine project. He and his classes have been filmed by TVO and Global's Kids-TV; featured in all local media - newspapers, TV, radio, as well as nationally in Reader's Digest, Toronto Star, Globe & Mail, Today's Parent, Home and Educational Computing and internationally on WGN and NPR radio, websites and dozens of student newspapers worldwide.

Made in the USA
Las Vegas, NV
01 December 2020